Introduction to Early Childhood Education

Join us on the Web at

EarlyChildEd.delmar.com

Introduction to Early Childhood Education

Linda Aulgur

Australia • Canada • Mexico • Singapore • Spain • United Kingdom • United States

TABLE OF CONTENTS

This tool was developed to help you, the budding teacher and/or child care provider, as you move into your first classroom. The editors at Thomson Delmar Learning encourage and appreciate your feedback on this or any of our other products. Go to http://www.earlychilded. delmar.com and click on the "Professional Enhancement series feedback" link to let us know what you think.

INTRODUCTION

Throughout a college preparation program to become an early childhood educator, students take many courses and read many textbooks. Their knowledge grows as they accumulate ideas from lectures, reading, experiences, and discussions. When they finish their coursework, graduate, and move into their first teaching positions, students often leave behind some of the books they have used. The hope is, however, that they take with them the important ideas from their classes and books as they begin their own professional practice.

More experienced colleagues or mentors sometimes support teachers in their first teaching positions, helping them make the transition from the college classroom to being responsible for a group of young children. Other times, new teachers are left to travel their own paths, relying on their own resources. Whatever your situation, this professional enhancement guide is designed to provide reminders of what you have learned, as well as resources to help you make sense of and apply that knowledge.

Teachers of young children are under great pressure today. Families demand support in their difficult tasks of child-rearing in today's fast-paced and changing world. Some families become so overwhelmed with the tasks of parenting that they seem to leave too much responsibility on the shoulders of teachers and caregivers. From administrators and institutions, there are expectations that sometimes seem overwhelming. Teachers are being held accountable for children's learning in ways unprecedented in even the recent past. Public scrutiny has led to insistence on teaching practices that may seem contrary to the best interests of children or their teachers. New teachers may find themselves caught between the realities of the schools or centers where they are working, and their own philosophies and ideals of working with children. When faced with such dilemmas, these individuals need to be able to fall back and reflect on what they know of best practices, renewing their professional determination to make appropriate decisions for children.

This book provides similar tools for that reflection:

- Tips for getting off to a great start in your new environment

- Information about typical developmental patterns of children from birth through school age

- Suggestions for materials that promote development for children from infancy through the primary grades

- Tools to assist teachers in observing children and gathering data to help set appropriate goals for individual children

- Guides for planning appropriate classroom experiences and sample lesson plans

- Tips for introducing children to the joys of literacy

- A summary of the key ideas about developmentally appropriate practice, the process of decision-making that allows teachers to provide optimum environments for children from birth through school age

- Professional development resources for teachers

- Ideas for locating lists of other resources

- Case studies of relevant, realistic situations you may face, as well as best practices for successfully navigating them

- Insight into issues and trends facing early childhood educators today

Becoming a teacher is a continuing process of growing, learning, reflecting, and discovering through experience. Having these resources will help you along your way. Good luck on your journey!

REFLECTIONS FOR GROWING TEACHERS

Teachers spend most of their time working with young children and their families. During the day, questions and concerns arise and decisions have to be made, meaning teachers must always be reflective about their work. Too often, teachers believe they are too busy to spend time thinking, but experienced professional teachers have learned that reflection sustains their best work. Growing teachers need to take time on a regular basis to consider the questions and concerns that arise from their practice. Some teachers use journals to keep track of the process.

Use these questions to begin your reflection and then add questions from your own experience. Remember, these are not questions to be answered once and forgotten, so come back often.

QUESTIONS FOR REFLECTION

This day would have been better if _____

_____.

I think I need to know more about _____

_____.

One new thing I think I'll try this week is _____

_____.

The highlight of this week was _____

_____.

The observations this week made me think more about _____

_____.

I think my favorite creative activity this year was _____

_____.

One area where my teaching is changing is _____

_____.

One area where my teaching needs to change is _____

_____.

I just don't understand why _____

_____.

I loved my job this week when _____

_____.

I hated my job this week when _____

_____.

One thing I can try to make better next week is _____

_____.

The funniest thing I heard a child say this week was _____

_____.

The family member I feel most comfortable with is _____

_____.

And I think the reason for that is _____

_____.

The family member I feel least comfortable with is _____

_____.

And I think the reason for that is _____

_____.

The biggest gains in learning have been made by _____

_____.

And I think that this is because _____

_____.

I'm working on a bad habit of _____

_____.

Has my attitude about teaching changed this year? Why? _____

_____.

What have I done lately to spark the children's imagination and creativity? _____

_____.

One quote that I like to keep in mind is _____

_____.

Dealing with _____ is the most difficult thing I had to face recently
because _____

_____.

My teaching style has been most influenced by _____

_____.

In thinking more about science, math, literacy, arts, and/or social studies in my curriculum, I believe _____

_____.

If I were going to advise a new teacher, the most helpful piece of advice would be

_____

_____.

I've been trying to facilitate friendships among the children by _____

_____.

I really need to start _____

_____.

I used to _____ but now I _____

_____.

The child who has helped me learn the most is _____. I learned

_____

_____.

I've grown in my communication by _____

_____.

The best thing I've learned by observing is _____

_____.

I still don't understand why _____

_____.

One mistake I used to make that I don't make any longer is _____

_____.

When next year starts, one thing I will do more of is _____

_____.

When next year starts, one thing I won't do is _____

_____.

One way I can help my children feel more competent is _____

_____.

Something I enjoy that I could share with my class is _____

_____.

When children have difficulty sharing, I _____

_____.

Adapted from Nilsen, B. A., *Week by Week: Documenting the Development of Young Children,*
3E, published by Thomson Delmar Learning.

TIPS FOR SUCCESS

Remember that you are a role model for the children. They are constantly watching how you dress, what you say, and what you do.

BE A PROFESSIONAL

- Dress conservatively and follow your employer's clothing expectations (which could include wearing closed-toe shoes to be safe and active with children and wearing clean, modest, and comfortable clothing).

- Be prepared and on time.

- Avoid excessive absences.

- Use appropriate language with children and adults.

- Be positive when talking to parents and show that you are forming a positive relationship with their children; "catch children doing something right" and share those accomplishments. Challenges with children can be discussed after you have established trust with the parents.

BE A TEAM PLAYER

- Rely on team members to help you learn the parameters of your new position.

- Don't be afraid to ask questions or request guidance from teammates.

- Show your support and be responsible.

- Step in to do your share of the work; don't expect others to clean up after you.

- Assist others whenever possible.

- Respect others' ideas and avoid telling them how to do things.

- Strive to balance your ability to make decisions with following the lead of others.

LEARN ABOUT CHILDREN

- Be aware of children's development physically, socially, emotionally, and cognitively.

- Assess children's development and plan curriculum that will enhance it.

- Be aware that children will test you! (Children, especially school age, will expect that you don't know the rules and may try to convince you to let them do things that were not previously allowed.)

- Never hesitate to double-check something with teammates when in doubt.

- Use positive management techniques with children.

MANAGEMENT TECHNIQUES FOR GAINING CHILDREN'S COOPERATION

Myriad techniques are useful for helping children cooperate. Children need respectful reminders of expectations and adult support to help them perform to those expectations. Be sure that your expectations are age appropriate and individually appropriate. These techniques are more preventive in nature:

- Use positive phrases and state exactly what you expect children to do. "Stand by the door" is more effective than "Don't go outside until everyone is ready."

- Avoid "no" and "don't." Be clear about what you want children to do, not what you don't want them to do.

- Sequence your directions by using "When-then" phrasing; for example, "When things are put away where they belong, then we can go outside."

- Stay close. Merely standing near children can be enough to help them manage behavior. Be aware, however, that if you are talking to another adult, children may act out because they know they do not have your attention.

- Offer sufficient and appropriate choices. Children need a variety of activities that interest them and that will create opportunities for success.

GETTING STARTED

When starting in a new position working with children, there is always an array of information to learn. Use this fill-in-the blank section to customize this resource book to your specific environment.

What are the school's or center's hours of operation?

On school days: _____

_____

_____

On vacation days: _____

_____

_____

What is the basic daily schedule and what are my responsibilities during each time segment?

_____

_____

_____

_____

_____

_____

_____

What are the procedures for checking children in and out of the program?

_____

_____

Do I call if I must be absent? Who is my contact?

Name: _____

Phone number: _____

What is the dress code for employees?

_____

_____

For what basic health and safety practices will I be responsible? Where are the materials stored?

Sanitizing tables: _____

_____

_____

_____

Cleaning and maintaining equipment and materials (bleach, gloves, and so on):

_____

_____

_____

What are the emergency procedures?

Mildly injured child: _____

_____

_____

_____

Earthquake/tornado: _____

_____

_____

_____

_____

_____

Fire: _____

_____

_____

_____

_____

_____

First aid: _____

_____

_____

_____

_____

Other: _____

_____

_____

_____

_____

DEVELOPMENTAL MILESTONES BY AGE

Whether you are working with infants, toddlers, preschoolers, or primary-aged children, your first requirement is to know how children develop and learn. In your college program, you no doubt studied child development. The following is a short-ened version of the universal steps most children go through as they develop. Some children move easily from one step to another, whereas other children move forward in one area but lag behind in others. Use these milestones as a guide for arranging an environment or planning activities in your room.

Child's Name _____   Age _____

Observer _____   Date _____

Developmental Checklist (by six months)

Does the child . . .	Yes	No	Sometimes
1. Show continued gains in height, weight, and head circumference?	☐	☐	☐
2. Reach for toys or objects when they are presented?	☐	☐	☐
3. Begin to roll from stomach to back?	☐	☐	☐
4. Sit with minimal support?	☐	☐	☐
5. Transfer objects from one hand to the other?	☐	☐	☐
6. Raise up on arms, lifting head and chest, when placed on stomach?	☐	☐	☐
7. Babble, coo, and imitate sounds?	☐	☐	☐
8. Turn to locate the source of a sound?	☐	☐	☐
9. Focus on an object and follow its movement vertically and horizontally?	☐	☐	☐

Developmental Checklist, continued			
Does the child ...	Yes	No	Sometimes
10. Exhibit a blink reflex?	☐	☐	☐
11. Enjoy being held and cuddled?	☐	☐	☐
12. Recognize and respond to familiar faces?	☐	☐	☐
13. Begin sleeping six to eight hours through the night?	☐	☐	☐
14. Suck vigorously when it is time to eat?	☐	☐	☐
15. Enjoy playing in water during bath time?	☐	☐	☐

DEVELOPMENTAL ALERTS

Check with a health care provider or early childhood specialist if, by *one month* of age, the infant *does not*

- show alarm or "startle" responses to loud noise.

- suck and swallow with ease.

- show gains in height, weight, and head circumference.

- grasp with equal strength with both hands.

- make eye-to-eye contact when awake and being held.

- become quiet soon after being picked up.

- roll head from side to side when placed on stomach.

- express needs and emotions with cries and patterns of vocalizations that can be distinguished from one another.

- stop crying when picked up and held.

DEVELOPMENTAL ALERTS

Check with a health care provider or early childhood specialist if, by four months of age, the infant *does not*

- continue to show steady increases in height, weight, and head circumference.

- smile in response to the smiles of others (the social smile is a significant developmental milestone).

- follow a moving object with eyes focusing together.

- bring hands together over mid-chest.

- turn head to locate sounds.

- begin to raise head and upper body when placed on stomach.

- reach for objects or familiar persons.

Child's Name _____ Age _____

Observer _____ Date _____

Developmental Checklist (by 12 months)

Does the child . . .	Yes	No	Sometimes
1. Walk with assistance?	☐	☐	☐
2. Roll a ball in imitation of an adult?	☐	☐	☐
3. Pick objects up with thumb and forefinger?	☐	☐	☐
4. Transfer objects from one hand to the other?	☐	☐	☐
5. Pick up dropped toys?	☐	☐	☐
6. Look directly at adult's face?	☐	☐	☐
7. Imitate gestures: peek-a-boo, bye-bye, pat-a-cake?	☐	☐	☐
8. Find object hidden under a cup?	☐	☐	☐
9. Feed self crackers (munching, not sucking on them)?	☐	☐	☐
10. Hold cup with two hands; drink with assistance?	☐	☐	☐
11. Smile spontaneously?	☐	☐	☐
12. Pay attention to own name?	☐	☐	☐
13. Respond to "no"?	☐	☐	☐
14. Respond differently to strangers and familiar persons?	☐	☐	☐
15. Respond differently to sounds: vacuum, phone, door?	☐	☐	☐
16. Look at person who speaks to him or her?	☐	☐	☐
17. Respond to simple directions accompanied by gestures?	☐	☐	☐
18. Make several consonant–vowel combination sounds?	☐	☐	☐
19. Vocalize back to person who has talked to him or her?	☐	☐	☐
20. Use intonation patterns that sound like scolding, asking, exclaiming?	☐	☐	☐
21. Say "da-da" or "ma-ma"?	☐	☐	☐

DEVELOPMENTAL ALERTS

Check with a health care provider or early childhood specialist if, by *twelve months* of age, the infant *does not*

- blink when fast-moving objects approach the eyes.
- begin to cut teeth.
- imitate simple sounds.
- follow simple verbal requests: "come", "bye-bye".
- pull self to a standing position.

Child's Name _____   Age _____

Observer _____   Date _____

Developmental Checklist (by two years)

Does the child . . .	Yes	No	Sometimes
1. Walk alone?	☐	☐	☐
2. Bend over and pick up toy without falling over?	☐	☐	☐
3. Seat self in child-size chair? Walk up and down stairs with assistance?	☐	☐	☐
4. Place several rings on a stick?	☐	☐	☐
5. Place five pegs in a pegboard?	☐	☐	☐
6. Turn pages two or three at a time?	☐	☐	☐
7. Scribble?	☐	☐	☐
8. Follow one-step direction involving something familiar: "Give me _____" "Show me _____" "Get a _____"?	☐	☐	☐
9. Match familiar objects?	☐	☐	☐
10. Use spoon with some spilling?	☐	☐	☐
11. Drink from cup holding it with one hand, unassisted?	☐	☐	☐
12. Chew food?	☐	☐	☐
13. Take off coat, shoe, sock?	☐	☐	☐
14. Zip and unzip large zipper?	☐	☐	☐
15. Recognize self in mirror or picture?	☐	☐	☐
16. Refer to self by name?	☐	☐	☐
17. Imitate adult behaviors in play—for example, feeds "baby"?	☐	☐	☐

Developmental Checklist, continued

Does the child . . .	Yes	No	Sometimes
18. Help put things away?	☐	☐	☐
19. Respond to specific words by showing what was named: toy, pet, family member?	☐	☐	☐
20. Ask for desired items by name: (for example, cookie)?	☐	☐	☐
21. Answer with name of object when asked "What's that"?	☐	☐	☐
22. Make some two-word statements: "Daddy bye-bye"?	☐	☐	☐

DEVELOPMENTAL ALERTS

Check with a health care provider or early childhood specialist if, by *twenty four months* of age, the child *does not*

- attempt to talk or repeat words.

- understand some new words.

- respond to simple questions with "yes" or "no."

- walk alone (or with very little help).

- exhibit a variety of emotions: anger, delight, fear.

- show interest in pictures.

- recognize self in mirror.

- attempt self-feeding: hold own cup to mouth and drink.

Child's Name _____   Age _____

Observer _____   Date _____

Developmental Checklist (by three years)

Does the child . . .	Yes	No	Sometimes
1. Run well in a forward direction?	☐	☐	☐
2. Jump in place, two feet together?	☐	☐	☐
3. Walk on tiptoe?	☐	☐	☐
4. Throw ball (but without direction or aim)?	☐	☐	☐
5. Kick ball forward?	☐	☐	☐
6. String four large beads?	☐	☐	☐

Developmental Checklist, continued			
Does the child . . .	**Yes**	**No**	**Sometimes**
7. Turn pages in book singly?	☐	☐	☐
8. Hold crayon: imitate circular, vertical, horizontal strokes?	☐	☐	☐
9. Match shapes?	☐	☐	☐
10. Demonstrate number concepts of 1 and 2?; (Can select 1 or 2; can tell if one or two objects.)	☐	☐	☐
11. Use spoon without spilling?	☐	☐	☐
12. Drink from a straw?	☐	☐	☐
13. Put on and take off coat?	☐	☐	☐
14. Wash and dry hands with some assistance?	☐	☐	☐
15. Watch other children; play near them; sometimes join in their play?	☐	☐	☐
16. Defend own possessions?	☐	☐	☐
17. Use symbols in play—for example, tin pan on head becomes helmet and crate becomes a spaceship?	☐	☐	☐
18. Respond to "Put _____ in the box," "Take the _____ out of the box"?	☐	☐	☐
19. Select correct item on request: big versus little; one versus two?	☐	☐	☐
20. Identify objects by their use: show own shoe when asked, "What do you wear on your feet?"	☐	☐	☐
21. Ask questions?	☐	☐	☐
22. Tell about something with functional phrases that carry meaning: "Daddy go airplane"; "Me hungry now"?	☐	☐	☐

DEVELOPMENTAL ALERTS

Check with a health care provider or early childhood specialist if, by the *third* birthday, the child *does not*

- eat a fairly well-rounded diet, even though amounts are limited.

- walk confidently with few stumbles or falls; climb steps with help.

- avoid bumping into objects.

- carry out simple, two-step directions: "Come to Daddy and bring your book"; express desires; ask questions.

- point to and name familiar objects; use two- or three-word sentences.

- enjoy being read to.

- show interest in playing with other children: watching, perhaps imitating.

- indicate a beginning interest in toilet training.

- sort familiar objects according to a single characteristic, such as type, color, or size.

Child's Name _____ Age _____

Observer _____ Date _____

Developmental Checklist (by four years)

Does the child . . .	Yes	No	Sometimes
1. Walk on a line?	☐	☐	☐
2. Balance on one foot briefly? Hop on one foot?	☐	☐	☐
3. Jump over an object 6 inches high and land on both feet together?	☐	☐	☐
4. Throw ball with direction?	☐	☐	☐
5. Copy circles and X's?	☐	☐	☐
6. Match six colors?	☐	☐	☐
7. Count to five?	☐	☐	☐
8. Pour well from pitcher? Spread butter, jam with knife?	☐	☐	☐
9. Button, unbutton large buttons?	☐	☐	☐
10. Know own sex, age, last name?	☐	☐	☐
11. Use toilet independently and reliably?	☐	☐	☐
12. Wash and dry hands unassisted?	☐	☐	☐
13. Listen to stories for at least five minutes?	☐	☐	☐
14. Draw head of person and at least one other body part?	☐	☐	☐
15. Play with other children?	☐	☐	☐
16. Share, take turns (with some assistance)?	☐	☐	☐
17. Engage in dramatic and pretend play?	☐	☐	☐
18. Respond appropriately to "Put it beside," "Put it under"?	☐	☐	☐
19. Respond to two-step directions: "Give me the sweater and put the shoe on the floor"?	☐	☐	☐

Developmental Checklist, continued			
Does the child ...	Yes	No	Sometimes
20. Respond by selecting the correct object—for example, hard versus soft object?	☐	☐	☐
21. Answer "if," "what," and "when" questions?	☐	☐	☐
22. Answer questions about function: "What are books for"?	☐	☐	☐

DEVELOPMENTAL ALERTS

Check with a health care provider or early childhood specialist if, by the *fourth* birthday, the child *does not*

- have intelligible speech most of the time; have children's hearing checked if there is any reason for concern.
- understand and follow simple commands and directions.
- state own name and age.
- enjoy playing near or with other children.
- use three- to four-word sentences.
- ask questions.
- stay with an activity for three or four minutes; play alone several minutes at a time.
- jump in place without falling.
- balance on one foot, at least briefly.
- help with dressing self.

FIVE- TO SEVEN-YEAR-OLDS

- More independent of parents, able to take care of their own physical needs
- Rely upon their peer group for self-esteem, have two or three best friends
- Learn to share and take turns, participate in group games
- Are eager to learn and succeed in school
- Have a sense of duty and develop a conscience
- Are less aggressive and resolve conflicts with words
- Begin to see others' point of view

- Can sustain interest for long periods of time
- Can remember and relate past events
- Have good muscle control and can manage simple tools
- Have a high energy level

Child's Name _____   Age _____

Observer _____   Date _____

Developmental Checklist (by five years)

Does the child . . .	Yes	No	Sometimes
1. Walk backward, heel to toe?	☐	☐	☐
2. Walk up and down stairs, alternating feet?	☐	☐	☐
3. Cut on line?	☐	☐	☐
4. Print some letters?	☐	☐	☐
5. Point to and name three shapes?	☐	☐	☐
6. Group common related objects: shoe, sock, and foot; apple, orange, and plum?	☐	☐	☐
7. Demonstrate number concepts to four or five?	☐	☐	☐
8. Cut food with a knife: celery, sandwich?	☐	☐	☐
9. Lace shoes?	☐	☐	☐
10. Read from story picture book—in other words, tell story by looking at pictures?	☐	☐	☐
11. Draw a person with three to six body parts?	☐	☐	☐
12. Play and interact with other children; engage in dramatic play that is close to reality?	☐	☐	☐
13. Build complex structures with blocks or other building materials?	☐	☐	☐
14. Respond to simple three-step directions: "Give me the pencil, put the book on the table, and hold the comb in your hand"?	☐	☐	☐
15. Respond correctly when asked to show penny, nickel, and dime?	☐	☐	☐
16. Ask "How" questions?	☐	☐	☐
17. Respond verbally to "Hi" and "How are you"?	☐	☐	☐
18. Tell about event using past and future tenses?	☐	☐	☐
19. Use conjunctions to string words and phrases together—for example, "I saw a bear and a zebra and a giraffe at the zoo"?	☐	☐	☐

DEVELOPMENTAL ALERTS

Check with a health care provider or early childhood specialist if, by the *fifth* birthday, the child *does not*

- state own name in full.

- recognize simple shapes: circle, square, triangle.

- catch a large ball when bounced (have child's vision checked).

- speak so as to be understood by strangers (have child's hearing checked).

- have good control of posture and movement.

- hop on one foot.

- appear interested in, and responsive to, surroundings.

- respond to statements without constantly asking to have them repeated.

- dress self with minimal adult assistance; manage buttons, zippers.

- take care of own toilet needs; have good bowel and bladder control with infrequent accidents.

Child's Name _____   Age _____

Observer _____   Date _____

Developmental Checklist (by six years)

Does the child . . .	Yes	No	Sometimes
1. Walk across a balance beam?	☐	☐	☐
2. Skip with alternating feet?	☐	☐	☐
3. Hop for several seconds on one foot?	☐	☐	☐
4. Cut out simple shapes?	☐	☐	☐
5. Copy own first name?	☐	☐	☐
6. Show well-established handedness; demonstrate consistent right- or left-handedness?	☐	☐	☐
7. Sort objects on one or more dimensions: color, shape, or function?	☐	☐	☐
8. Name most letters and numerals?	☐	☐	☐
9. Count by rote to 10; know what number comes next?	☐	☐	☐

| **Developmental Checklist, continued** | | | |
Does the child ...	Yes	No	Sometimes
10. Dress self completely; tie bows?	☐	☐	☐
11. Brush teeth unassisted?	☐	☐	☐
12. Have some concept of clock time in relation to daily schedule?	☐	☐	☐
13. Cross street safely?	☐	☐	☐
14. Draw a person with head, trunk, legs, arms, and features; often add clothing details?	☐	☐	☐
15. Play simple board games?	☐	☐	☐
16. Engage in cooperative play with other children, involving group decisions, role assignments, rule observance?	☐	☐	☐
17. Use construction toys, such as plastic interlocking blocks, blocks, to make recognizable structures?	☐	☐	☐
18. Do 15-piece puzzles?	☐	☐	☐
19. Use all grammatical structures: pronouns, plurals, verb tenses, conjunctions?	☐	☐	☐
20. Use complex sentences: carry on conversations?	☐	☐	☐

DEVELOPMENTAL ALERTS

Check with a health care provider or early childhood specialist if, by the *sixth* birthday, the child *does not*

- alternate feet when walking up and down stairs.
- speak in a moderate voice; neither too loud, too soft, too high, too low.
- follow simple directions in stated order: "Please go to the cupboard, get a cup, and bring it to me."
- use four to five words in acceptable sentence structure.
- cut on a line with scissors.
- sit still and listen to an entire short story (five to seven minutes).
- maintain eye contact when spoken to (unless this is a cultural taboo).
- play well with other children.
- perform most self-grooming tasks independently: brush teeth, wash hands and face.

Child's Name _____   Age _____

Observer _____   Date _____

Developmental Checklist (by seven years)

Does the child ...	Yes	No	Sometimes
1. Concentrate on completing puzzles and board games?	☐	☐	☐
2. Ask many questions?	☐	☐	☐
3. Use correct verb tenses, word order, and sentence structure in conversation?	☐	☐	☐
4. Correctly identify right and left hands?	☐	☐	☐
5. Make friends easily?	☐	☐	☐
6. Show some control of anger, using words instead of physical aggression?	☐	☐	☐
7. Participate in play that requires teamwork and rule observance?	☐	☐	☐
8. Seek adult approval for efforts?	☐	☐	☐
9. Enjoy reading and being read to?	☐	☐	☐
10. Use pencil to write words and numbers?	☐	☐	☐
11. Sleep undisturbed through the night?	☐	☐	☐
12. Catch a tennis ball, walk across a balance beam, hit a ball with a bat?	☐	☐	☐
13. Plan and carry out simple projects with minimal adult help?	☐	☐	☐
14. Tie own shoes?	☐	☐	☐
15. Draw pictures with greater detail and sense of proportion?	☐	☐	☐
16. Care for own personal needs with some adult supervision? Wash hands? Brush teeth? Use toilet? Dress self?	☐	☐	☐
17. Show some understanding of cause-and-effect concepts?	☐	☐	☐

DEVELOPMENTAL ALERTS

Check with a health care provider or early childhood specialist if, by the *seventh* birthday, the child *does not*

- show signs of ongoing growth, including increasing height and weight and continuing motor development, such as running, jumping, balancing.

- show some interest in reading and trying to reproduce letters, especially own name.

- follow simple, multiple-step directions: "Finish your book, put it on the shelf, and then get your coat on."

- follow through with instructions and complete simple tasks: putting dishes in the sink, picking up clothes, finishing a puzzle. (*Note:* All children forget. Task incompletion is not a problem unless a child *repeatedly* leaves tasks unfinished.)

- begin to develop alternatives to excessive use of inappropriate behaviors in order to get own way.

- develop a steady decrease in tension-type behaviors that may have developed with starting school: repeated grimacing or facial tics, eye twitching, grinding teeth, regressive soiling or wetting, frequent stomachaches, refusing to go to school.

8- TO 10-YEAR-OLDS

- Need parental guidance and support for school achievement.

- Competition is common.

- Pronounced gender differences in interests; same gender cliques formed.

- Spend a lot of time in physical game playing.

- Academic achievement is important.

- Begin to develop moral values, make value judgments about own behavior.

- Are aware of the importance of belonging.

- Strong gender role conformation.

- Begin to think logically and to understand cause and effect.

- Use language to communicate ideas and can use abstract words.

- Can read, but ability varies.

- Realize importance of physical skills in determining status among peers.

Child's Name _____   Age _____
Observer _____   Date _____

Developmental Checklist (by eight and nine years)

Does the child . . .	Yes	No	Sometimes
1. Have energy to play, continuing growth, few illnesses?	☐	☐	☐
2. Use pencil in a deliberate and controlled manner?	☐	☐	☐
3. Express relatively complex thoughts in a clear and logical fashion?	☐	☐	☐
4. Carry out multiple four- to five-step instructions?	☐	☐	☐
5. Become less easily frustrated with own performance?	☐	☐	☐
6. Interact and play cooperatively with other children?	☐	☐	☐
7. Show interest in creative expression—telling stories, telling jokes, writing, drawing, singing?	☐	☐	☐
8. Use eating utensils with ease?	☐	☐	☐
9. Have a good appetite? Show interest in trying new foods?	☐	☐	☐
10. Know how to tell time?	☐	☐	☐
11. Have control of bowel and bladder functions?	☐	☐	☐
12. Participate in some group activities—games, sports, plays?	☐	☐	☐
13. Want to go to school? Seem disappointed if must miss a day?	☐	☐	☐
14. Demonstrate beginning skills in reading, writing, and math?	☐	☐	☐
15. Accept responsibility and complete work independently?	☐	☐	☐
16. Handle stressful situations without becoming overly upset?	☐	☐	☐

DEVELOPMENTAL ALERTS

Check with a health care provider or early childhood specialist if, by the *eighth* birthday, the child *does not*

- attend to the task at hand; show longer periods of sitting quietly, listening, responding appropriately.
- follow through on simple instructions.
- go to school willingly most days (of concern are excessive complaints about stomachaches or headaches when getting ready for school).

- make friends (observe closely to see if the child plays alone most of the time or withdraws consistently from contact with other children).

- sleep soundly most nights (frequent and recurring nightmares or bad dreams are usually at a minimum at this age).

- seem to see or hear adequately at times (squints, rubs eyes excessively, asks frequently to have things repeated).

- handle stressful situations without undue emotional upset (excessive crying, sleeping or eating disturbances, withdrawal, frequent anxiety).

- assume responsibility for personal care (dressing, bathing, feeding self) most of the time.

- show improved motor skills.

DEVELOPMENTAL ALERTS

Check with a health care provider or early childhood specialist if, by the *ninth* birthday, the child *does not*

- exhibit a good appetite and continued weight gain (some children, especially girls, may already begin to show early signs of an eating disorder).

- experience fewer illnesses.

- show improved motor skills, in terms of agility, speed, and balance.

- understand abstract concepts and use complex thought processes to problem-solve.

- enjoy school and the challenge of learning.

- follow through on multiple-step instructions.

- express ideas clearly and fluently.

- form friendships with other children and enjoy participating in group activities.

11- TO 13-YEAR-OLDS

- Parental influence is decreasing and some rebellion may occur.

- Peer group is important and sets standards for behavior.

- Worry about what others think.

- Choose friends based on common interests.

- Gender differences in interests.

- Develop awareness and interest in opposite gender.

- Begin to question adult authority.

- Often reluctant to attend child care; are bored or think they can care for themselves.

- May be moody and experience stress over physical changes of puberty.

- May be rebellious as they seek their own identity.

- Can think abstractly and apply logic to solving problems.

- Have a good command of spoken and written language.

- Develop gender characteristics (girls); begin a growth spurt (boys).

- Early maturing is related to a positive self-image.

- Able to master physical skills necessary for playing games.

Child's Name _____   Age _____

Observer _____   Date _____

Developmental Checklist (by 11 to 13 years)

Does the child . . .	Yes	No	Sometimes
1. Continue to increase in height and weight?	☐	☐	☐
2. Exhibit improving coordination: running, climbing, riding a bike, writing?	☐	☐	☐
3. Handle stressful situations without becoming overly upset or violent?	☐	☐	☐
4. Construct sentences using reasonably correct grammar: nouns, adverbs, verbs, adjectives?	☐	☐	☐

Developmental Checklist, continued

Does the child . . .	Yes	No	Sometimes
5. Understand concepts of time, distance, space, volume?	☐	☐	☐
6. Have one or two "best friends"?	☐	☐	☐
7. Maintain friendships over time?	☐	☐	☐
8. Approach challenges with a reasonable degree of self-confidence?	☐	☐	☐
9. Play cooperatively and follow group instructions?	☐	☐	☐
10. Begin to show an understanding of moral standards: right from wrong, fairness, honesty, good from bad?	☐	☐	☐
11. Look forward to, and enjoy, school?	☐	☐	☐
12. Appear to hear well and listen attentively?	☐	☐	☐
13. Enjoy reasonably good health, with few episodes of illness or health-related complaints?	☐	☐	☐
14. Have a good appetite and enjoy mealtimes?	☐	☐	☐
15. Take care of own personal hygiene without assistance?	☐	☐	☐
16. Sleep through the night, waking up refreshed and energetic?	☐	☐	☐

DEVELOPMENTAL ALERTS

Check with a health care provider or early childhood specialist if, by the *eleventh* birthday, the child *does not*

- continue to grow at a rate appropriate for the child's gender.

- show continued improvement of fine motor skills.

- make or keep friends.

- enjoy going to school and show interest in learning (have children's hearing and vision tested; vision and hearing problems affect children's ability to learn and their interest in learning).

- approach new situations with reasonable confidence.

- handle failure and frustration in a constructive manner.

- sleep through the night or experience prolonged problems with bedwetting, nightmares, or sleepwalking.

Child's Name _____   Age _____
Observer _____   Date _____

Developmental Checklist (by 12 and 13 years)

Does the child . . .	Yes	No	Sometimes
1. Appear to be growing: increasing height and maintaining a healthy weight (not too thin or too heavy)?	☐	☐	☐
2. Understand changes associated with puberty or have an opportunity to learn and ask questions?	☐	☐	☐
3. Complain of headaches or blurred vision?	☐	☐	☐
4. Have an abnormal posture or curving of the spine?	☐	☐	☐
5. Seem energetic and not chronically fatigued?	☐	☐	☐
6. Stay focused on a task and complete assignments?	☐	☐	☐
7. Remember and carry out complex instructions?	☐	☐	☐
8. Sequence, order, and classify objects?	☐	☐	☐
9. Use longer and more complex sentence structure?	☐	☐	☐
10. Engage in conversation; tell jokes and riddles?	☐	☐	☐
11. Enjoy playing organized games and team sports?	☐	☐	☐
12. Respond to anger-invoking situations without resorting to violence or physical aggression?	☐	☐	☐
13. Begin to understand and solve complex mathematical problems?	☐	☐	☐
14. Accept blame for actions on most occasions?	☐	☐	☐
15. Enjoy competition?	☐	☐	☐
16. Accept and carry out responsibility in a dependable manner?	☐	☐	☐
17. Go to bed willingly and wake up refreshed?	☐	☐	☐
18. Take pride in appearance; keep self reasonably clean?	☐	☐	☐

DEVELOPMENTAL ALERTS

Check with a health care provider or early childhood specialist if, by the *thirteenth* birthday, the child *does not*

- have movements that are smooth and coordinated.
- have energy sufficient for playing, riding bikes, or engaging in other desired activities.

- stay focused on tasks at hand.

- understand basic cause-and-effect relationships.

- handle criticism and frustration with a reasonable response (physical aggression and excessive crying could be an indication of other, underlying problems).

- exhibit a healthy appetite (frequent skipping of meals is not typical for this age group).

- make and keep friends.

Some content in this section adapted from Allen, E. A., and Marotz, L., *Developmental Profiles: Pre-birth through Twelve,* 4E, published by Thomson Delmar Learning.

DEVELOPMENTAL MILESTONES BY SKILL

As with the list of milestones by age, this list is not exhaustive, but it can be used to arrange an environment or to plan activities in your room.

BIRTH TO ONE MONTH

Physical	Date Observed
Engages in primarily reflexive motor activity	
Maintains "fetal" position especially when sleeping	
Holds hands in a fist; does not reach for objects	
In prone position, head falls lower than the body's horizontal line with hips flexed and arms and legs hanging down	
Has good upper body muscle tone when supported under the arms	
Cognitive	
Blinks in response to fast-approaching object	
Follows a slowly moving object through a complete 180-degree arc	
Follows objects moved vertically if close to face	
Continues looking about, even in the dark	
Begins to study own hand when lying in tonic neck reflex position	
Prefers to listen to mother's voice rather than a stranger's	
Language	
Cries and fusses as major forms of communication	
Reacts to loud noises by blinking, moving (or stopping), shifting eyes, making a startle response	
Shows preference for certain sounds (music and human voices) by calming down or quieting	
Turns head to locate voices and other sounds	
Makes occasional sounds other than crying	
Social/Emotional	
Experiences a short period of alertness immediately following birth	
Sleeps 17–19 hours a day; is gradually awake and responsive for longer periods	
Likes to be held close and cuddled when awake	

Social/Emotional, continued	Date Observed
Shows qualities of individuality in responding or not responding to similar situations	
Begins to establish emotional attachment or bonding with parents and caregivers	
Begins to develop a sense of security/trust with parents and caregivers; responses to different individuals vary	

ONE TO FOUR MONTHS

Physical	Date Observed
Rooting and sucking reflexes are well developed	
In prone position, Landau reflex appears and baby raises head and upper body on arms	
Grasps with entire hand; strength insufficient to hold items	
Movements tend to be large and jerky	
Turns head side to side when in a supine (face up) position	
Begins rolling from front to back by turning head to one side and allowing trunk to follow	
Cognitive	
Fixes on a moving object held at 12 inches (30.5 cm)	
Continues to gaze in direction of moving objects that have disappeared	
Exhibits some sense of size/color/shape recognition of objects in the immediate environment	
Alternates looking at an object, at one or both hands, and then back at the object	
Moves eyes from one object to another	
Focuses on small object and reaches for it; usually follows own hand movements	
Language	
Reacts to sounds (voice, rattle, doorbell); later will search for source by turning head	
Coordinates vocalizing, looking, and body movements in face-to-face exchanges with parent or caregiver	
Babbles or coos when spoken to or smiled at	
Imitates own sounds and vowel sounds produced by others.	
Laughs out loud	
Social/Emotional	
Imitates, maintains, terminates, and avoids interactions	
Reacts differently to variations in adult voices	

Social/Emotional, continued	Date Observed
Enjoys being held and cuddled at times other than feeding and bedtime	
Coos, gurgles, and squeals when awake	
Smiles in response to a friendly face or voice	
Entertains self for brief periods by playing with fingers, hands, and toes	

FOUR TO EIGHT MONTHS

Physical	Date Observed
Parachute reflex appears toward the end of this stage; swallowing reflex appears	
Uses finger and thumb (pincer grip) to pick up objects	
Reaches for objects with both arms simultaneously; later reaches with one hand	
Transfers objects from one hand to the other; grasps object using palmar grasp	
Handles, shakes, and pounds objects; puts everything in mouth	
Sits alone without support (holds head erect, back straight, arms propped forward for support)	
Cognitive	
Turns toward and locates familiar voices and sounds	
Uses hand, mouth, and eyes in coordination to explore own body, toys, and surroundings	
Imitates actions, such as pat-a-cake, waving bye-bye, and playing peek-a-boo	
Shows fear of falling from high places, such as changing table, stairs	
Looks over side of crib or high chair for objects dropped; delights in repeatedly throwing objects overboard for adult to retrieve	
Bangs objects together playfully; bangs spoon or toy on table	
Language	
Responds appropriately to own name and simple requests, such as "eat," "wave bye-bye"	
Imitates some nonspeech sounds, such as cough, tongue click, lip smack	
Produces a full range of vowels and some consonants: r, s, z, th, and w	
Responds to variations in the tone of voice of others	
Expresses emotions (pleasure, satisfaction, anger) by making different sounds	
Babbles by repeating same syllable in a series: ba, ba, ba.	
Social/Emotional	
Delights in observing surroundings; continuously watches people and activities	
Begins to develop an awareness of self as a separate individual from others	
Becomes more outgoing and social in nature: smiles, coos, reaches out	

Social/Emotional, continued	Date Observed
Distinguishes among, and responds differently, to strangers, teachers, parents, siblings	
Responds differently and appropriately to facial expressions: frowns, smiles	
Imitates facial expressions, actions, and sounds	

8 TO 12 MONTHS

Physical	Date Observed
Reaches with one hand leading to grasp an offered object or toy	
Manipulates objects, transferring them from one hand to the other	
Explores new objects by poking with one finger	
Uses deliberate pincer grip to pick up small objects, toys, and finger foods	
Stacks objects; also places objects inside one another	
Releases objects by dropping or throwing; cannot intentionally put an object down	
Begins pulling self to a standing position; begins to stand alone	
Cognitive	
Watches people, objects, and activities in the immediate environment	
Shows awareness of distant objects (15 to 20 feet away) by pointing at them	
Reaches for toys that are visible but out of reach	
Continues to drop first item when other toys or items are offered	
Recognizes the reversal of an object: cup upside down is still a cup	
Imitates activities: hitting two blocks together, playing pat-a-cake	
Language	
Babbles or jabbers to initiate social interaction; may shout to attract attention	
Shakes head for "no" and may nod for "yes"	
Responds by looking for voice when name is called	
Babbles in sentence-like sequences; followed by jargon (syllables/sounds with language-like inflection)	
Waves "bye-bye"; claps hands when asked	
Says "da-da" and "ma-ma"	
Social/Emotional	
Exhibits a definite fear of strangers; clings to, or hides behind, parent or caregiver ("stranger anxiety"); resists separating from familiar adult ("separation anxiety")	
Enjoys being near, and included in, daily activities of family members and teachers; is becoming more sociable and outgoing	

Social/Emotional, continued	Date Observed
Enjoys novel experiences and opportunities to examine new objects	
Shows need to be picked up and held by extending arms upward, crying, or clinging to adult's legs	
Begins to exhibit assertiveness by resisting caregiver's requests; may kick, scream, or throw self on the floor	

ONE-YEAR-OLDS

Physical	Date Observed
Crawls skillfully and quickly; gets to feet unaided	
Stands alone with feet spread apart, legs stiffened, and arms extended for support	
Walks unassisted near the end of this period (most children); falls often; not always able to maneuver around furniture or toys	
Uses furniture to lower self to floor; collapses backward into a sitting position or falls forward on hands and then sits	
Releases an object voluntarily	
Enjoys pushing or pulling toys while walking	
Cognitive	
Enjoys object-hiding activities: early on, will search same location for a hidden object; later will search in several locations	
Passes toy to other hand when offered a second object ("crossing the midline")	
Manages three to four objects by setting an object aside (on lap or floor) when presented with a new toy	
Puts toys in mouth less often	
Enjoys looking at picture books	
Demonstrates understanding of functional relationships (objects that belong together)	
Language	
Produces considerable "jargon": combines words/sounds into speech-like patterns	
Uses one word to convey an entire thought (holophrastic speech); later, produces two-word phrases to express a complete thought (telegraphic speech)	
Follows simple directions: "Give Daddy the cup"	
Points to familiar persons, animals, and toys when asked	
Identifies three body parts if someone names them: "Show me your nose (toe, ear)"	
Indicates a few desired objects/activities by name: "bye-bye," "cookie"; verbal request is often accompanied by an insistent gesture	

Social/Emotional	Date Observed
Remains friendly toward others; usually less wary of strangers	
Helps pick up and put away toys	
Plays alone for short periods and does not play cooperatively	
Enjoys being held and read to	
Imitates adult actions in play	
Enjoys adult attention; likes to know that an adult is near; gives hugs and kisses	

TWO-YEAR-OLDS

Physical	Date Observed
Walks with a more erect, heel-to-toe pattern; can maneuver around obstacles in pathway	
Runs with greater confidence; has fewer falls	
Squats for long periods while playing	
Climbs stairs unassisted (but not with alternating feet)	
Balances on one foot (for a few moments), jumps up and down, but may fall	
Begins to achieve toilet training (depending on physical and neurological development) although accidents should still be expected; will indicate readiness for toilet training	
Cognitive	
Exhibits better coordinated eye–hand movements; can put objects together, take them apart; fit large pegs into pegboard	
Begins to use objects for purposes other than intended (pushes block around as boat)	
Completes classification based on one dimension (separates toy dinosaurs from toy cars)	
Stares for long moments; seems fascinated by, or engrossed in, figuring out a situation	
Attends to self-selected activities for longer periods of time	
Shows discovery of cause and effect: squeezing the cat makes her scratch	
Language	
Enjoys being read to if allowed to point, make relevant noises, turn pages	
Realizes that language is effective for getting others to respond to needs and preferences	
Uses 50 to 300 different words; vocabulary continuously increasing	
Has broken linguistic code; in other words, much of a two-year-old's talk has meaning to him or her	

Language, continued	Date Observed
Understands more language than can communicate verbally; most two-year-olds' receptive language is more developed than their expressive language	
Utters three- and four-word statements; uses conventional word order to form more complete sentences	
Social/Emotional	
Shows empathy and caring	
Continues to use physical aggression if frustrated or angry (more exaggerated in some children); physical aggression lessens as verbal skills improve	
Expresses frustration through temper tantrums; tantrum frequency peaks during this year; cannot be reasoned with while tantrum is in progress	
Finds it difficult to wait or take turns; often impatient	
Enjoys "helping" with household chores; imitates everyday activities	
Orders parents and teachers around; makes demands and expects immediate compliance	

THREE-YEAR-OLDS

Physical	Date Observed
Walks up and down stairs unassisted using alternating feet; may jump from bottom step, landing on both feet	
Balances momentarily on one foot	
Kicks a large ball, catches a large bounced ball with both arms extended	
Feeds self; needs minimal assistance	
Jumps in place	
Pedals a small tricycle or other mobile toy	
Cognitive	
Listens attentively and makes relevant comments during age-appropriate stories, especially those related to home and family events	
Likes to look at books and may pretend to "read" to others or explain pictures	
Enjoys stories with riddles, guessing, and suspense	
Points with fair accuracy to correct pictures when given sound-alike words: keys–cheese; fish–dish; mouse–mouth	
Plays realistically: feeds doll; hooks truck and trailer together	
Places 8 to 10 pegs in pegboard, or 6 round and 6 square blocks in form board	
Language	
Talks about objects, events, and people not present: "Jerry has a pool in his yard"	
Talks about the actions of others: "Daddy's mowing the grass"	

Language, continued	Date Observed
Adds information to what has just been said: "Yeah, and then he grabbed it back"	
Answers simple questions appropriately	
Asks increasing numbers of questions, including location/identity of objects and people	
Uses increased speech forms to keep conversation going: "What did he do next?" "How come she hid?"	
Social/Emotional	
Seems to understand taking turns, but not always willing to do so	
Laughs frequently; is friendly and eager to please	
Has occasional nightmares and fears the dark, monsters, or fire	
Joins in simple games and group activities, sometimes hesitantly	
Talks to self often	
Uses objects symbolically in play: block of wood may be a truck, a ramp, a bat	

FOUR-YEAR-OLDS

Physical	Date Observed
Walks a straight line (tape or chalkline on the floor)	
Hops on one foot	
Pedals and steers a wheeled toy with confidence; avoids obstacles and oncoming "traffic"	
Climbs ladders, trees, playground equipment	
Jumps over objects 5 or 6 inches (12.5 to 15 cm) high; lands with both feet together	
Runs, starts, stops, and moves around obstacles with ease	
Cognitive	
Stacks at least five graduated cubes largest to smallest; builds a pyramid of six blocks	
Indicates if paired words sound the same or different: sheet–feet, ball–wall	
Names 18–20 uppercase letters near the end of this year; may be able to print several and write own name; may recognize some printed words (especially those that have special meaning)	
May begin to read simple books (alphabet books with few words per page and many pictures)	
Likes stories about how things grow and operate	
Delights in wordplay, creating silly language	

Language	Date Observed
Uses the prepositions "on," "in," and "under"	
Uses possessives consistently: "hers," "theirs," "baby's"	
Answers "Whose?" "Who?" "Why?" and "How many?"	
Produces elaborate sentence structures	
Uses almost entirely intelligible speech	
Begins to correctly use the past tense of verbs: "Mommy closed the door," "Daddy went to work."	
Social/Emotional	
Is outgoing and friendly; overly enthusiastic at times	
Changes moods rapidly and unpredictably; often throws tantrum over minor frustrations; sulks over being left out	
Holds conversations and shares strong emotions with imaginary playmates or companions; invisible friends are common	
Boasts, exaggerates, and "bends" the truth with made-up stories or claims; tests limits with "bathroom" talk	
Cooperates with others; participates in group activities	
Shows pride in accomplishments; seeks frequent adult approval	

FIVE-YEAR-OLDS

Physical	Date Observed
Walks backward, heel to toe	
Walks unassisted up and down stairs, alternating feet	
Learns to turn somersaults (should be taught the right way to avoid injury)	
Touches toes without flexing knees	
Catches a ball thrown from 3 feet away	
Rides a tricycle or wheeled toy with speed and skillful steering; some learn to ride bicycles, usually with training wheels	
Cognitive	
Forms rectangle from two triangular cuts	
Builds steps with set of small blocks	
Understands concept of same shape, same size	
Sorts objects on the basis of two dimensions, such as color and form	
Sorts objects so that all things in the group have a single common feature	
Understands smallest and shortest; places objects in order from shortest to tallest, smallest to largest	

Language	Date Observed
Has vocabulary of 1,500 words or more	
Tells a familiar story while looking at pictures in a book	
Uses functional definitions: a ball is to bounce; a bed is to sleep in	
Identifies and names four to eight colors	
Recognizes the humor in simple jokes; makes up jokes and riddles	
Produces sentences with five to seven words; much longer sentences are not unusual	
Social/Emotional	
Enjoys friendships; often has one or two special playmates	
Shares toys, takes turns, plays cooperatively (with occasional lapses); is often quite generous	
Participates in play and activities with other children; suggests imaginative and elaborate play ideas	
Is affectionate and caring, especially toward younger or injured children and animals	
Follows directions and carries out assignments usually; generally does what parent or teacher requests	
Continues to need adult comfort and reassurance, but may be less open in seeking and accepting comfort	

SIX-YEAR-OLDS

Physical	Date Observed
Has increased muscle strength; typically boys are stronger than girls of similar size	
Gains greater control over large and fine motor skills; movements are more precise and deliberate although some clumsiness persists	
Enjoys vigorous physical activity: running, jumping, climbing, and throwing	
Moves constantly, even when trying to sit still	
Has increased dexterity, eye–hand coordination, and improved motor functioning, which facilitate learning to ride a bicycle, swim, swing a bat, or kick a ball	
Enjoys art projects: likes to paint, model with clay, "make things," draw and color, work with wood	
Cognitive	
Shows increased attention; works at tasks for longer periods, although concentrated effort is not always consistent	
Understands simple time markers (today, tomorrow, yesterday) or uncomplicated concepts of motion (cars go faster than bicycles)	
Recognizes seasons and major holidays and the activities associated with each	

Cognitive, continued	Date Observed
Enjoys puzzles, counting and sorting activities, paper-and-pencil mazes, and games that involve matching letters and words with pictures	
Recognizes some words by sight; attempts to sound out words (some may read well by this time)	
Identifies familiar coins: pennies, nickels, dimes, quarters	
Language	
Loves to talk, often nonstop; may be described as a chatterbox	
Carries on adult-like conversations; asks many questions	
Learns 5 to 10 new words daily; vocabulary consists of 10,000 to 14,000 words	
Uses appropriate verb tenses, word order, and sentence structure	
Uses language (not tantrums or physical aggression) to express displeasure: "That's mine! Give it back, you dummy."	
Talks self through steps required in simple problem-solving situations (although the "logic" may be unclear to adults)	
Social/Emotional	
Experiences mood swings: "best friends" then "worst enemies"; loving then uncooperative and irritable; especially unpredictable toward mother or primary caregiver	
Becomes less dependent on parents as friendship circle expands; still needs closeness and nurturing but has urges to break away and "grow up"	
Needs and seeks adult approval, reassurance, and praise; may complain excessively about minor hurts to gain more attention	
Continues to be egocentric; still sees events almost entirely from own perspective: views everything and everyone as there for child's own benefit	
Easily disappointed and frustrated by self-perceived failure	
Has difficulty composing and soothing self; cannot tolerate being corrected or losing at games; may sulk, cry, refuse to play, or reinvent rules to suit own purposes	

SEVEN-YEAR-OLDS

Physical	Date Observed
Exhibits large and fine motor control that is more finely tuned	
Tends to be cautious in undertaking more challenging physical activities, such as climbing up or jumping down from high places	
Practices a new motor skill repeatedly until mastered then moves on to something else	
Finds floor more comfortable than furniture when reading or watching television; legs often in constant motion	

Physical, continued	Date Observed
Uses knife and fork appropriately, but inconsistently	
Tightly grasps pencil near the tip; rests head on forearm, lowers head almost to the table top when doing pencil-and-paper tasks	
Cognitive	
Understands concepts of space and time in both logical and practical ways: a year is "a long time"; 100 miles is "far away"	
Begins to grasp Piaget's concepts of conservation (the shape of a container does not necessarily reflect what it can hold)	
Gains a better understanding of cause and effect: "If I'm late for school again, I'll be in big trouble"	
Tells time by the clock and understands calendar time—days, months, years, seasons	
Plans ahead: "I'm saving this cookie for tonight"	
Shows marked fascination with magic tricks; enjoys putting on "shows" for parents and friends	
Language	
Enjoys storytelling; likes to write short stories, tell imaginative tales	
Uses adult-like sentence structure and language in conversation; patterns reflect cultural and geographical differences	
Becomes more precise and elaborate in use of language; greater use of descriptive adjectives and adverbs	
Uses gestures to illustrate conversations	
Criticizes own performance: "I didn't draw that right," "Her picture is better than mine"	
Verbal exaggeration commonplace: "I ate 10 hot dogs at the picnic"	
Social/Emotional	
Is cooperative and affectionate toward adults and less frequently annoyed with them; sees humor in everyday happenings	
Likes to be the "teacher's helper"; eager for teacher's attention and approval but less obvious about seeking it	
Seeks out friendships; friends are important, but can stay busy if no one is available	
Quarrels less often, although squabbles and tattling continue in both one-on-one and group play	
Complains that family decisions are unjust, that a particular sibling gets to do more or is given more	
Blames others for own mistakes; makes up alibis for personal shortcomings: "I could have made a better one, but my teacher didn't give me enough time"	

EIGHT-YEAR-OLDS

Physical	Date Observed
Enjoys vigorous activity; likes to dance, roller blade, swim, wrestle, bicycle, fly kites	
Seeks opportunities to participate in team activities and games: soccer, baseball, kickball	
Exhibits significant improvement in agility, balance, speed, and strength	
Copies words and numbers from blackboard with increasing speed and accuracy; has good eye–hand coordination	
Possesses seemingly endless energy	
Cognitive	
Collects objects; organizes and displays items according to more complex systems; bargains and trades with friends to obtain additional pieces	
Saves money for small purchases; eagerly develops plans to earn cash for odd jobs; studies catalogs and magazines for items to purchase	
Begins taking an interest in what others think and do; understands there are differences of opinion, cultures, distant countries	
Accepts challenge and responsibility with enthusiasm; delights in being asked to perform tasks at home and in school; interested in being rewarded	
Likes to read and work independently; spends considerable time planning and making lists	
Understands perspective (shadow, distance, shape); drawings reflect more realistic portrayal of objects	
Language	
Delights in telling jokes and riddles	
Understands and carries out multiple-step instructions (up to five steps); may need directions repeated because of not listening to the entire request	
Enjoys writing letters or sending e-mail messages to friends; includes imaginative and detailed descriptions	
Uses language to criticize and compliment others; repeats slang and curse words	
Understands and follows rules of grammar in conversation and written form	
Is intrigued with learning secret word codes and using code language	
Converses fluently with adults; can think and talk about past and future: "What time are we leaving to get to the swim meet next week?"	
Social/Emotional	
Begins forming opinions about moral values and attitudes; declares things right or wrong	
Plays with two or three "best" friends, most often the same age and gender; also enjoys spending some time alone	

Social/Emotional, continued	Date Observed
Seems less critical of own performance but is easily frustrated when unable to complete a task or when the product does not meet expectations	
Enjoys team games and activities; values group membership and acceptance by peers	
Continues to blame others or makes up alibis to explain own shortcomings or mistakes	
Enjoys talking on the telephone with friends	

Some content in this section adapted from Allen, E. A., and Marotz, L., *Developmental Profiles: Pre-birth through Twelve*, 4E, published by Thomson Delmar Learning.

PLAY MATERIALS FOR CHILDREN

Children construct their own understanding of the world around them as they interact with appropriate materials and with other people. Teachers play an important role in providing choices of good-quality playthings that match children's developmental abilities and interests. When budgets are limited, teachers must be able to select toys and materials that provide optimum learning opportunities. Creative teachers learn how to "scrounge" for toys and how to make playthings out of recycled materials.

CRITERIA FOR SELECTING PLAY EQUIPMENT FOR YOUNG CHILDREN

A young child's playthings should be as free of detail as possible.

- Too much detail hampers a child's freedom to express himself or herself.

- "Unstructured" toys, which allow the imagination free rein, include blocks, construction sets, clay, sand, and paints.

A good plaything should stimulate children to do things for themselves.

- Equipment that makes the child a spectator may entertain but has little or no play value.

- Play equipment should encourage children to explore and create or offer dramatic play potential.

Young children need large, easily manipulated playthings.

- Toys too small can be frustrating because the child's undeveloped muscular coordination cannot handle smaller forms and shapes.

■ A child's muscles develop through play, so equipment should allow for climbing and balancing.

The material of which a plaything is constructed has an important role in the play of the young child.

■ Warmth and pleasurable touch are significant (wood and cloth are the most satisfactory materials)

■ The plaything's durability is of utmost importance.

■ Play materials must be sturdy; axles and wheels must be able to support a child's weight.

■ Children hate to see their toys break.

■ Some materials break readily, which makes them expensive.

The toy must "work."

■ Be sure parts move correctly.

■ Make sure maintenance will be easy.

A plaything's construction should be simple enough for a child to comprehend.

■ This strengthens the child's understanding and experience of the world.

■ Mechanics should be visible and easily grasped; small children will take playthings apart to see how they tick.

A plaything should encourage cooperative play.

■ Provide an environment that stimulates children to work and play together.

The total usefulness of the plaything must be considered in comparing price.

■ Will it last several children through several stages of their playing lives?

The lists that follow suggest the materials that are priorities for children at particular levels of development.

FOR YOUNG INFANTS BIRTH THROUGH SIX MONTHS

- unbreakable mirrors that can be attached low on walls or near changing tables and cribs
- stuffed, washable toys or rag dolls, with stitched faces and eyes
- mobiles and visuals hung out of reach
- grasping toys: simple rattles, squeeze toys, keys on ring, clutch or texture balls
- hanging toys for batting
- wrist or ankle bells

FOR OLDER, MOBILE INFANTS 7 THROUGH 12 MONTHS

- soft rubber animals for grasping
- simple one-piece vehicles 6–8 inches, with large wheels
- grasping toys for skill development: toys on suction cups, stacking rings, nesting cups, squeeze toys, plastic pop beads, bean bags, busy boxes
- containers and objects to fill and dump
- small cloth, plastic, and board books
- soft cloth or foam blocks for stacking
- simple floating objects for water play
- balls of all kinds, including some with special effects
- low, soft climbing platforms
- large unbreakable mirrors
- infant swings for outdoors
- recorded music and songs

FOR TODDLERS ONE TO THREE YEARS

For Fine Motor Skills

- nesting materials
- sand and water play toys: funnels, colanders, small sand tools

- simple activity boxes, with doors, lids, switches, more complex after about 18 months: turning knob or key

- pegboards with large pegs

- four- or five-piece stacking materials

- pop beads and stringing beads

- simple three- to five-piece puzzles with knobs, familiar shapes

- simple matching materials

- books, including tactile books, cloth, plastic, and board picture books

For Gross Motor Skills

- push and pull toys

- simple doll carriages and wagons

- stable riding toys with four wheels and no pedals

- balls of all sizes

- tunnels for crawling through

- tumbling mats and low climbing platforms

For Pretend Play

- small wood or plastic people and animal figures

- small cars and trucks

- dolls

- plastic dishes and pots and pans

- doll beds

- hats

- simple dress-ups

- telephones

- scarves and fabrics

For Sensory Play

- recorded music and player

- play dough

- fingerpaint
- large nontoxic crayons
- sturdy paper
- simple musical instruments

FOR CHILDREN THREE THROUGH FIVE

For Gross Motor Play

- small wagons and wheelbarrows
- replications of adult tools for pushing and pretend play, such as lawn mower, shopping cart
- scooters
- tricycles and other vehicles with steering ability
- riding toys for more than one child
- balls of all sizes, especially 10-inch and 12-inch balls for kicking and throwing
- hollow plastic bat and lightweight ball
- jump rope
- stationary outdoor climbing equipment
- slides and ladders
- outdoor building materials, tires, and other loose parts

Exploration and Mastery Play Materials

- sand and water play: measures, funnels, tubes, sand tools
- construction materials: unit blocks, large hollow blocks
- Legos®-type plastic interlocking blocks
- puzzles, including fit-in puzzles and large, simple jigsaw puzzles, with varying numbers of pieces, according to children's age
- pattern-making materials: beads for stringing, pegboards, mosaic boards, feltboards, color cubes
- dressing, lacing, and stringing: sewing cards and dressing frames

- collections of small plastic objects for matching, sorting, and ordering by color, shape, size, or other category concepts

- simple, concrete number materials for counting and matching to numerals

- measuring materials: scales, measuring cups for liquids

- science materials: magnifying glass, color paddles, objects from the natural world, including pets

- beginning computer programs

- games: dominoes; lotto games; bingo by color, number, or picture; first board games that use concepts such as color or counting; memory

- books of all kinds: picture books, realistic stories, alphabet picture books, poetry, information books

- writing center materials: clipboards, colored pencils, old calendars, envelopes, notepads, stationery, rubber stamps and ink pads, rulers, magnetic letters, stencil shapes, stickers, file cards, and office materials

For Pretend Play

- dolls of various ethnic and gender appearance, with clothes and other accessories and furniture

- housekeeping equipment

- variety of dress-ups, including those related to various roles and themes

- transportation toys

- hand puppets

- animal and human figures for play scenes

- full-length, unbreakable mirror

For Creative Play

- art and craft materials: crayons, markers, easel, paintbrushes, paint and fingerpaint, varieties of paper, chalkboard and chalk, safety scissors, glue, collage materials, clay and play dough, and tools to use with them

- workbench with hammer, saw, and nails

- musical instruments

- recorded music for singing, movement and dancing, listening, and for using with rhythm instruments

FOR CHILDREN SIX THROUGH EIGHT YEARS

For Gross Motor Play

- balls and sports equipment for beginning team play, such as soccer, baseball

- complex climbing structures: ropes, ladders, rings, hanging bars

- materials for target practice

- mats for acrobatics

- bicycles and scooters

For Exploration and Mastery Play

- construction materials for large constructions and for creating models, including metal parts and nuts and bolts

- puzzles: 100-piece jigsaw puzzles, three-dimensional puzzles such as Rubik's cubes

- craft materials for braiding, weaving, knitting, leather craft, jewelry making, sewing

- pattern-making materials: mosaic tiles, geometric puzzles

- games: word games, simple card games, reading and spelling games, number and counting games, beginning strategy games such as checkers

- materials for specific learning: printing materials, math manipulatives, measuring materials, science materials, and computer programs for language arts, number and concept development, and for problem-solving activities

- books at a variety of levels for beginning readers—see the Resources list on page 87.

For Creative Activities

- variety of markers, colored pencils, chalks, paintbrushes and paints, art papers for tracing and drawing

- clay and tools, including pottery wheel

- workbench with wood and variety of tools

- real instruments such as guitars and recorders

- music for singing and movement

- audiovisual materials for independent use

Some ideas adapted from Bronson, M., *The Right Stuff for Children Birth to 8: Selecting Play Materials to Support Development*, published by NAEYC.

Unconventional Materials

Remember that recycled materials and other loose parts have many uses for exploration and creativity. These materials can be valuable tools in a number of curriculum areas:

- Empty plastic containers: detergent bottles, bleach bottles, old refrigerator containers, which can be used for constructing scoops, storing art materials, and so on.

- Buttons—all colors and sizes—are excellent for collages, assemblages, as well as sorting, counting, matching, and so on.

- Egg shells, which can be washed, dried, and colored with food coloring for art projects.

- Coffee or shortening cans and lids, which can be covered with adhesive paper and used for storage of art supplies, games, and manipulatives materials.

- Magazines with colorful pictures, which are excellent for making collages, murals, and posters.

- Scraps of fabric: felt, silk, cotton, oil cloth, and so on, which can be used to make "fabric boards" with the name of each fabric written under a small swatch attached to the board, as well as for collages, puppets, and more.

- Yarn scraps, which can be used for separating buttons into sets; also for art activities.

- Styrofoam scraps.

- Scraps of lace, rick rack, or decorative trim.

- Bottles with sprinkler tops, which are excellent for water play and for mixing water as children fingerpaint.

- Wallpaper books of discontinued patterns.

- Paper doilies.

- Discarded wrapping paper.

- Paint color cards from paint/hardware stores.

- Old paintbrushes.

- Old jewelry and beads.

- Old muffin tins, which are effective for sorting small objects and mixing paint.

- Tongue depressors or ice cream sticks, which can be used as counters for math and are good for art construction projects, stick puppets, and so on.

- Wooden clothespins, which can be used for making "people," for construction projects, and for hanging up paintings to dry.

Adapted from Mayesky, M., *Creative Activities for Young Children*, 7E, published by Thomson Delmar Learning.

BASIC PROGRAM EQUIPMENT AND MATERIALS FOR AN EARLY CHILDHOOD CENTER

If you are responsible for ordering supplies for your classroom or early childhood program, the following guidelines will be useful.

INDOOR EQUIPMENT

The early childhood room should be arranged into well-planned areas of interest, such as the housekeeping and doll corner, block building area, and so on to encourage children to play in small groups throughout the playroom, engaging in activities of their special interest, rather than attempting to play in one large group.

The early childhood center must provide selections of indoor play equipment from many areas of interest. Selection should be of sufficient quantities so that children can participate in a wide range of activities. Many pieces of equipment can be homemade. Consider the age and developmental levels of the children when making selections.

Playroom Furnishings

- *Tables:* seat four to six children (18 inches high for three-year-olds, 20–22-inches high for four- and five-year-olds)

- *Chairs:* 10 inches high for three-year-olds, 12–14 inches high for four- and five-year-olds

- *Open shelves:* 26 inches high, 12 inches deep, 12 inches between shelves

- *Lockers:* 12 inches wide, 12 inches deep, 32–36 inches high

Housekeeping or Doll Corner

Item	Number Recommended for 10 Children
Dolls	3
Doll clothes	Variety
Doll bed—should be large enough for a child to get into, bedding	1
Doll high chair	1
Small table, four chairs	1 set
Tea party dishes	6-piece set with tray
Stove: child size, approximately 24 × 23 × 12 inches	1
Sink: child size, approximately 24 × 23 × 12 inches	1
Refrigerator: child size, approximately 28 × 23 × 12 inches	1
Pots and pans, empty food cartons, measuring cups, spoons, and so on	Variety
Mop, broom, dustpan	1
Ironing board and iron	1
Clothespins and clothesline	1
Toy telephones	2
Dress-up box—men's and women's hats, neckties, pocketbooks, shoes, old dresses, scarves, jewelry, and so on	Variety
Mirror	1

Art Supplies

Item	Number Recommended for 10 Children
Newsprint paper 18 × 24 inches	1 ream
Colored paper—variety	3 packages
Large crayons	10 boxes
Tempera paint—red, yellow, blue, black, white	1 can each
Long-handled paintbrushes: making a stroke from ½ inch to 1 inch wide	10–12
Easels	1
Fingerpaint paper: glazed paper such as shelf, freezer, or butcher's paper	1 roll
Paste	1 quart
Blunt scissors	10
Collage: collection of bits of colored paper, cut-up gift wrappings, ribbons, cotton, string, scraps of fabric, and so on for pasting	Variety
Magazines for cutting and pasting	Variety

Item, continued	Number Recommended for 10 Children
Clay: play dough	50 pounds
Cookie cutters, rolling pins	Variety
Smocks or aprons to protect children's clothes	10

Block Building Area

Item	Number Recommended for 10 Children
Unit blocks: purchased or homemade (directions are available)	276 pieces, 11 shapes
Large, lightweight blocks	Variety
Small wooden or rubber animals and people	Variety
Small trucks, airplanes, cars, and boats	12
Medium airplanes	3
Medium boats	2
Medium-sized trucks: 12 to 24 inches	3

Music Corner

- record player, tape player, CD player
- suitable records, tapes, and CDs
- rhythm instruments
- dress-up scarves for dancing

Manipulative Toys

Item	Number Recommended for 10 Children
Wooden inlay puzzles, approximately 5 to 20 pieces	6
Color cone	1
Nested blocks	1
Pegboards, variety of shapes and sizes	1
Large spools and beads for stringing	2 sets
Toys that have parts that fit into one another	2
Lotto games	2
Dominoes	1

Books and Stories

A carefully selected book collection (20–30 books) for the various age levels should include the following:

- transportation, birds and animals, family life
- community helpers, science, nonsense rhymes
- Mother Goose rhymes, poems, and stories
- homemade picture books
- collection of pictures classified by subject
- library books to enrich the collection

Nature Study and Science

- aquarium or fish bowls
- plastic materials
- magnifying glass, prism, magnet, thermometers
- growing indoor plants, garden plot
- stones, leaves, acorns, birds' nests, caterpillars, worms, tadpoles, and so on

Woodworking Center

Basic woodworking operations are

- sanding
- gluing
- hammering
- holding (with a vise or clamp)
- fastening (with screws)
- drilling
- sawing

Materials for a woodworking center include the following:

- sturdy workbench (or table)
- woodworking tools: broad-headed nails ¾ to 1½ inches long; C-clamp or vise (to hold wood); flat-headed, 12-oz. hammer for beginning woodworking experiences, later a

claw hammer may be added; 14-inch saw with 10 teeth to the inch

- soft white pine lumber scraps (it is difficult to drive nails into hardwood; plywood is not suitable either); packing boxes of soft pine can be disassembled and used for hammering work.

Sand Play

- For outdoors, sand should be confined so it is not scattered over the rest of the playground.

- Outdoor area should be large enough for several children to move about without crowding each other.

- A 10- to 12-inch ledge around a sandbox can serve as a boundary and provide children with a working surface or a seat.

- Keep sand to 6 to 8 inches below the top of the ledge so that it is less likely to spill out.

- Sand should be about 18 inches deep so children can dig or make tunnels.

- For drainage, include 4 or 5 inches of gravel on the bottom of the sandbox.

- Basic equipment: plastic or metal kitchen utensils, cups, spoons, pails, shovels, sifters, funnels, scoops, bowls.

Water Play

- Can be either indoor or outdoor activity, depending on climate.

- Can use clear plastic water basins on a stand with wheels to allow them to be moved to any area of a room.

- When using plastic basins, children can see through the sides and the bottom.

- For tables on a carpeted floor, use a plastic runner to protect the carpet.

- Materials: Clear tubing, sponges, strainers, funnels, corks, pitchers, and measuring cups; for added interest: rotary beaters, spoons, small bowls, plastic basters, and straws.

OUTDOOR EQUIPMENT

Outdoor play equipment should be grouped according to use. For example, plan for both active and quiet play; allow for free areas for use of wheel toys. Suggested basic outdoor play equipment for the early childhood program includes the following:

- climbing structure(s)

- large and small packing boxes

- slides

- swings with canvas seats

- wagons and wheelbarrows

- pedal toys: tricycles, cars, and so on

- sandbox with spoons, shovels, pails, and so on

- balls

- a variety of salvage materials: rubber tires, tire tubes, lengths of garden hose, ropes, and cardboard boxes

Note: Many activities, such as housekeeping play and art activities, at times can be transferred to the outdoor area.

Use this checklist to evaluate your playground setup:

☐ Pathways are clear and spacious enough between areas so that traffic flows well and equipment does not obstruct the children's movement.

☐ Space and equipment are organized so that children are readily visible and easily supervised by adults.

☐ Different activity areas are separated. (Tricycle paths are separate from the swings; the sandbox is separate from the climbing area.)

☐ Open space is available for active play.

☐ Some space is available for quiet play.

☐ Dramatic play can be set up outdoors, as space is available.

Procedure: Begin by talking about how trees look in the current season, and ask children how the tree will change in the next season, then the next, and so on (bare tree in winter, tiny buds in spring, full green leaves in summer, colored leaves falling in fall).

1. Pass out the paper.

2. Have the children fold the paper in half, and then in half again. Have them open the paper up. They should have four rectangles marked by the folded lines.

3. Tell the children to start with current season, drawing the tree in the first box, then drawing the tree again in the next box, detailing the change.

4. Pass out the markers and let the children begin to draw.

5. Display the pictures and have the children tell about their own.

This activity can be adapted to many different levels: older children can draw a house being constructed in four stages, younger children can draw a snowman or a jack o' lantern being built in four steps, or any other topic where there is a developmental sequence. Most ages will also enjoy drawing a baby, a child, a teenager, and an adult in the boxes, too.

TITLE OF LESSON OR ACTIVITY: NAME PATTERNS

Developmental Focus: Fine motor skills, literacy concepts, patterning, creativity

Goal: Children will trace around their names, noting shapes, and possibly using patterns.

Age Range: 6 to adult

Materials: White paper for each child, markers, colored pencils or crayons

Procedure:

1. Print (or write) your name on the board or demonstration paper and talk about the shapes of the letters; some extend below or above the main line most letters rest on. Use one color to trace completely around the letters, leaving a small

margin. Choose a different color and trace around the first line, leaving same amount of space. Explain that children will do the same, continuing to make lines extending all the way to the edges of the paper. Older children may want to repeat a color pattern.

2. Distribute materials.

3. Have younger children fold the paper in half lengthwise (like a hot dog bun), and open it up. Then they will have a line down the middle to write their name on.

TITLE OF LESSON OR ACTIVITY: CLOCK SOLITAIRE

Developmental Focus: Math skills, noncompetitive large group cooperation

Goal: Children will recognize numerals, use symbols for numerals, and form a clock face.

Age Range: Ages 5 to 7, works well for groups of 6 up to 24 children

Materials: A deck of cards

Procedure: Have children sit on floor in large circle. Explain that they are going to play Clock Solitaire, where they will try to beat the "bad kings." Pretend to draw a giant clock inside the circle, and note where the numbers would be on that clock by identifying children who are sitting close to that spot. (Example: "Joe and Meg are sitting where the 12 would be, and Ted and Jane are down here where the six would be.") Explain that a deck of cards doesn't have the same numbers as a clock, so the Ace represents 1, Jacks are 11, Queens are 12s, and the Kings are the bad cards.

Place the shuffled deck face down in the center of circle. The first child turns one card over, and places the card on the clock face to represent that number. If the child gets a King, it goes face up next to deck. If there is already a number card at a certain numeral place, the child can place another on top of it. (The three of hearts can be played on the three of spades, and so on.) Play continues around the circle, each child getting a turn. The goal is to get all 12 numerals represented before all four kings turn up in the deck. In that case, the class has "beaten the kings." Be prepared to play this over and over; it holds children's attention for a long time.

TITLE OF LESSON OR ACTIVITY: PAPER PLATE SPIDERS

Developmental Focus: Fine motor skills; Math number skills, 1–8

Goal: Children will construct spiders with eight legs.

Age Range: 4 to 6

Materials: Paper plates (any size); precut 1 × 23–inch strips of construction paper; tape, glue, or stapler to attach strips to plate; markers; and precut lengths of yarn or string to hang spiders by

Procedure: Sing the song "Eency Weency Spider" together. Talk about spider characteristics: They have eight legs, spin webs from single string, and have many eyes. Explain that the plate will be the spider's head, and children can draw eyes or fangs on the plate. Each child gets eight strips of paper, which he or she can count out on his or her own. Have children fold up one inch of each strip, and then show them how to turn it over, and fold the opposite way, another inch, then repeating until entire strip has been folded accordion style. This gives the legs a bumpy, jumpy effect. Attach the legs to the plate, letting children do as much as possible. Teacher should punch a small hole in center of plate and insert string, knotting it securely, and taping it in place. The child then can hold the spider by the string, or the spiders can be displayed hanging from the ceiling. Sing the song again. Have fun. (This project works well with an older child being paired with a younger child in a cooperative project.)

TITLE OF LESSON OR ACTIVITY: TORN PAPER COLLAGE LANDSCAPES

Developmental Focus: Fine motor, creativity, problem-solving

Goal: Students will tear small shapes of paper and glue onto a solid color sheet to make a picture.

Age Range: 8 and above

Materials: One sheet of paper for each child, large collection of different-colored scrap paper, and glue. No pencils or scissors allowed.

Procedure: Talk about or show pictures of mosaics. Review the art term "landscape." Let the children choose several scraps of paper and tell them they can make anything in their landscape, but it has to have at least three objects. Explain that they can't use scissors or draw with pencils. Caution them against tearing the paper into too tiny pieces.

Extension: Have children write a story about the place they have represented.

A number of Web sites offer sample lesson plans for teachers. When downloading lesson plans from the Internet or another source, be sure each plan lists the

- objective or goal of the lesson.
- materials needed.
- directions for the activity.
- appropriate age group.
- developmental appropriateness.

Check the Resources section of this manual for a list of Web sites with lesson plans and other free materials for teachers.

BOOKS FOR CHILDREN

Reading aloud is a wonderful gift you can give to children. Through sharing an interesting book, you introduce children to a world they might not otherwise be able to visit. Through books, you can travel anywhere you like, have experiences outside the realm of your current environment, participate in wonderful fantasies, and be saddened and then uplifted.

Children's desire to read and the ability to do so is fostered by reading to them as soon as they are born. Even babies can enjoy looking at picture books and hearing simple stories. Preschoolers love to have favorite books read to them repeatedly. As children move into the school years, they can sustain their interest in longer books that are divided into chapters. When they realize the joy that comes from good books, they are more motivated to read on their own.

Many textbooks provide suggestions for setting up reading corners and providing books for children to read by themselves. This section focuses on books that you can read aloud to children in small or large groups. Remember that the more you read, the better you will become at doing so. When the books have been enjoyed in a group setting, add them to the book corner for children to read alone. In addition, teachers often create lending arrangements where children can take home books for their parents to read and then return. Teachers who believe in the importance of reading choose the best of children's literature and involve families in reading.

HOW TO GET CHILDREN TO LISTEN AND WANT MORE

- Schedule time each day for reading, maybe toward the end of the day when children are tired and will enjoy the inactivity; make sure the setting is comfortable.

- Choose books that you also enjoy, perhaps one you read as a child; preview the book before presenting it to the children in case there are passages you want to shorten.

- The first time you read a book, state the title and author. Research for interesting facts about the author to share with the children. If there is an illustrator, include that information as well.

- If you are reading to a large group, position yourself so that you are slightly higher than the children so that your voice will project more easily.

- If you are reading to a small group, sit among children in a more intimate placement, which will draw them to you and the book.

- Occasionally stop and ask, "What do you think is going to happen next?"

- Read at a pace that allows children to build mental images of the characters or setting; change your pace to match the action of the story: slow your pace and lower your voice during a suspenseful spot and then speed up when the action does.

- Allow time for discussion only if children want to. Let them voice fears, ask questions, or share their thoughts about the book. Do not turn the discussion into a quiz or need to interpret the story.

- Practice reading aloud, trying to vary your expression or tone of voice.

- Create a display of images or information pertaining to the book you are reading. A map will allow children to pinpoint places mentioned in the story. Pictures, charts, or time lines will also add to the display. Objects or foods mentioned in the book add another dimension.

- Find a stopping place each day that will create suspense, so that the children are eager to get back to the book the next day.

- When you pick up the book the next day, ask children if they remember what had happened just before you stopped reading.

WHAT NOT TO DO

- Don't read a book you do not enjoy; your feelings will be sensed by the children.

- Don't read a book when it becomes obvious that it was a poor choice; previewing the book before presenting it to the children can minimize these kinds of mistakes.

- Don't choose a book with which some of the children are already familiar; they may have heard it at home or seen a version on television or at the movies.

- Don't start a book unless you have enough time to read more than a few pages.

- Don't be fooled by awards. Just because a book has received a national book award does not mean that it is suitable for your particular group of children.

- Don't impose on the children your own interpretations or reactions to the story. Let them express their own understanding and feelings.

GREAT READ-ALOUD BOOKS FOR VERY YOUNG PRESCHOOLERS

Chicka Boom Boom, Bill Martin, Jr, and John Archambault, illustrated by Lois Ehlert, Simon & Schuster, 1989.

Ages 2–5. 32 pages.

Rollicking lyrics about the vivid colored letters of the alphabet, as they climb coconut trees and do other surprising feats.

Rumble in the Jungle, Giles Andreae, illustrated by David Wojtowycz, Tiger Tales, 2001.

Ages 2–5. 32 pages.

Bright pastel illustrations of jungle animals are introduced in each two-page spread. The text is a long delightful predictable rhyme as the animals go on a journey through the jungle.

Ten, Nine, Eight, illustrated by Molly Bang, Greenwillow, 1996.

Ages 2–6. 24 pages.

A loving daddy puts his little girl to bed, making the routine seem exciting. Familiar words encourage language development and counting.

Fiddle-I-Fee, Will Hillenbrand, Harcourt, 2002.

Ages 2–5. 32 pages.

The old song has a modern twist in the illustrations, but the same lyrics. Children will enjoy "singing" the book with you, and then dramatizing it as well.

Glad Monster Sad Monster: A Book about Feelings, Ed Emberly and Ann Miranda. Little Brown and Company, 1997.

Ages 3–6. 16 pages.

Each black two-page spread opens out into an extra fold-out page that is a mask of the monster, depicting a particular emotion. Colors and objects are associated with each feeling, such as the blue monster waving good-bye and watching the snow monster melt.

BOOKS FOR OLDER PRESCHOOLERS, KINDERGARTEN, AND THE EARLY GRADES

The Grouchy Ladybug, Eric Carle, HarperCollins, 1996.

Ages 4–6. Approximately 22 pages.

A grouchy ladybug takes on bigger creatures than her as concepts about telling time are presented. This is a great book to have the children act out.

Gator Gumbo, Candace Fleming, illustrated by Sally Lambert. Farrar Straus Giroux, 2004.

Ages 4–8. 32 pages.

Repetitive key phrases in the tradition of the Gingerbread Boy or Little Red Hen, this story has the French Cajun surprise ending that delights listeners of all ages.

Boo to a Goose, Mem Fox, Hodder and Stoughton Children's Books, 1996.

Ages 4–8. 32 pages.

Striking collage illustrations entertain children along with the hilarious rhyming patterns on each page. This book can be used as a springboard for children to begin writing their own rhymes.

The Kissing Hand, Audrey Penn, illustrated by Ruth Harper and Nancy Leak, Scholastic, 1993.

Ages 4–6. 28 pages.

Chester Raccoon learns to leave his mother and go to school despite his apprehension. The book reassures children that they are loved even if they are not with their parents.

The Maestro Plays, Bill Martin, Jr., illustrated by Vladimir Radunsky, Scholastic, 1995.

Ages 3–8. 32 pages.

Brilliant abstract illustrations and flowing text highlight this book about a zany orchestra.

Yo! Yes?, Chris Raschka, Orchard Books, 1993.

Ages 4–7. 30 pages.

The single words and simple illustrations on each page describe a whole range of emotions as a shy boy is befriended by another boy who is a basketball player. Children develop empathy for the characters instantly.

BOOKS FOR OLDER ELEMENTARY GRADES

Zin! Zin! Zin! A Violin, Lloyd Moss, illustrated by Marjorie Priceman, Simon and Schuster, 1995.

Ages 6–8. 27 pages.

Brilliant folk art illustrations and text that is printed in curving lines take the listeners through the orchestra, teaching musical and number terms such as cello, valves, quartet, and reeds. The rhyming text is music itself.

The Paper Bag Princess, Robert Munsch, illustrated by Michael Martchenko, Annick Press, Ltd., 1980.

Ages 6–10. 24 pages.

This nontraditional fairy tale makes a case for strong females solving their own problems. Humorous take-off makes listeners think what "lived happily ever after" might mean to different individuals.

Just Another Ordinary Day, Rod Cement, HarperCollins, 1995.

Ages 6–10. 32 pages.

Amanda lives a highly unusual life in a most ordinary way. Outlandish vivid illustrations show her as she interacts with dinosaurs, aliens, and pirates, yet has a normal routine like most elementary school-aged children.

Aunt Chip and the Great Triple Creek Dam Affair, Patricia Polacco, Philomel Books, 1996.

Ages 7–11. 38 pages.

The town of Triple Creek is so caught up in watching TV that residents have forgotten what books are for. Eli solves the mystery of how this has happened, and gets the whole town reading again.

NOTES

98